How Things Work: The Computers

Table of Contents

Introduction 5

How do computers and technology work?
Introduction to Computers 7
A brief history of the computers 12
Basic Operations of a Computer 15
Types of Computers 20

The Computer
What are the Components of a Computer? 25
How does a Computer Work? 34

The Internet
What is the Internet? 39
How the Internet Works? 43
Common Internet Services 46

Security on the Internet
What is Internet Security? 57
Why is Internet Security Important? 59
Different Types of Security Threats 61
Protecting Yourself Online 64

Blockchain
What is Blockchain? 71

Benefits of Blockchain 75
Real-World Applications of Blockchain 78

Artificial Intelligence
What is Artificial Intelligence? 81
A brief history of AI 83
Types of Artificial Intelligence 85
Benefits of Artificial Intelligence 88
Real-World Applications of Artificial Intelligence ... 94

Closing Thoughts 101

Introduction

Welcome to the world of technology and computers, where the possibilities and advancements are limitless. In today's digital age, computers and technology have become integral to our daily lives, shaping how we communicate, work, and interact with the world around us. But for those who are not well-versed in the world of technology, understanding the inner workings of computers and how they operate can be an overwhelming task.

This book is designed to be a comprehensive guide for those new to computers and technology. It covers the basic concepts of computing and technology, including the computer, the internet, security on the internet, blockchain, and artificial intelligence.

The first part of the book explores the fundamental concepts of computers, including the basic components of a computer, how it works, and the different types of computers available in the market. It also covers the various operating systems and software applications that run on computers.

The second part of the book delves into the internet, which has transformed how we

communicate, learn, and interact. We will explore the history of the internet, how it works, and the different types of
online platforms and services available to us.

Our online data and personal information security is vital in today's digital age. The book's third part explores the different aspects of online security, including common threats, how to protect ourselves online, and the various tools and techniques available to safeguard our online data.

The fourth part of the book covers the revolutionary technology of blockchain, disrupting industries and changing the way we conduct transactions. We will explore the basics of blockchain, how it works, and the different types of applications of this technology.

Finally, the last part of the book will focus on one of the most exciting and groundbreaking fields in technology: artificial intelligence. We will explore the basic concepts of AI, the different types of AI, and how it is used in various industries and fields.

No matter why you want to learn about computers, this book is designed to help you better understand the different aspects of computers and technology.

How do computers and technology work?

Introduction to Computers

What is a computer?
A computer is an electronic device that can store, process, and retrieve information. At its most basic level, a computer has a central processing unit (CPU) that acts as the "brain" of the computer. This is where all the calculations and operations are performed. A computer also has memory (such as RAM) to store information and instructions for the CPU and a storage device (such as a hard drive) to store data and programs even when the computer is turned off.

A computer also has a variety of input and output devices, such as a keyboard, mouse, and monitor, that allow you to interact with the computer and see the results of your actions.

A computer can be used for many different purposes, from basic tasks like typing and browsing the web to more complex tasks like video editing and scientific simulations. And, because computers are constantly improving, they are becoming even more powerful and versatile, allowing us to do things we never thought possible just a few years ago!

What do computers do?

Computers are capable of performing a wide range of tasks, from simple to complex. Some of the most common tasks that computers can perform include:

- **Word Processing.** Computers can create, edit, and format documents, such as letters, resumes, and reports. This makes it easy to type and format your work and then print it or share it with others.
- **Internet Browsing.** Computers can connect to the internet. With a computer and an internet connection, you can use a web browser to visit websites, watch videos, listen to music, and more.
- **Email.** Computers can be used to send and receive emails. An email is an electronic form of communication that allows you to communicate with others quickly and easily. With an email account, you can send messages to friends and family and receive important messages from work or school.

- **Gaming.** Computers can also be used to play games. Many types of games are available for computers, from simple arcade-style games to complex role-playing games and everything in between.
- **Social Media.** You can connect with others through social media, which are websites and applications that allow you to share information and communicate with friends, family, and other people who share your interests. Some popular social media platforms include Facebook, Twitter, and Instagram.
- **Productivity.** Computers can be used for productivity, which means using the computer to get things done efficiently and effectively. This can include managing your finances, organizing your schedule, and keeping track of important information.
- **Education.** You could use the computer to learn new things and acquire new skills. This can include taking online courses, watching educational videos, and researching information for school projects.
- **Graphic Design.** Computers can create and manipulate images, illustrations, and other visual elements. With the right software, you can create beautiful and eye-catching designs, such as logos, posters, and web pages.

- **Music and Video.** You can use computers to edit music and video. You can create, edit, and enjoy music and video content. This can include recording and mixing music, editing video, and watching movies and TV shows.
- **Science and Engineering.** Computers can also be used for science and engineering, which involves using the computer to perform complex calculations and simulations. This can include modeling and analyzing data, predicting outcomes, and developing new technologies.

Why are computers important?

Computers are important because they make our lives easier and help us to accomplish tasks faster and more efficiently.

With the help of computers, we can complete tasks much more quickly and easily than we could before. For example, instead of writing a letter by hand, we can type it on a computer and send it through the internet in just a few seconds. This saves time and helps us be more productive in our jobs and personal lives.

Computers are like massive libraries that can store vast amounts of information. With just a few clicks, we can access information about almost any topic from anywhere in the world. We can use computers to communicate with others, stay connected with family and friends, no matter where they are in the world, and find new information every day. Doctors and other healthcare professionals use computers to store and manage patient information and keep track of medical treatments and procedures.

Furthermore computers help with medical research, allowing scientists to find new treatments and cures for diseases.

On top of that, they can also be a great source of entertainment. We can use computers to watch movies, play games, listen to music, and much more. This helps us to relax and have fun after a long day.

Computers have become an essential part of our lives. They help us be more productive, access information, have fun, improve healthcare, and stay connected with others. By understanding how computers work and how to use them effectively, we can make the most of them and continue to enjoy the many benefits they bring to our lives.

A brief history of the computers

Computers have become an integral part of modern society, and it is difficult to imagine a world without them. They are present in almost all areas of life, including education, business, entertainment, and communication. However, the modern computer has evolved over the centuries, and its history is fascinating.

The first computers were not electronic devices but rather mechanical. In the early 19th century, mathematician Charles Babbage designed and built the first mechanical computer called the Difference Engine. It was designed to compute tables of numbers automatically. Although it was never completed, it laid the foundation for modern computing.

In the early 20th century, electronic computers began to emerge. The first electronic computer was Colossus, built in 1943 by British engineer Tommy Flowers. It was used to decipher coded messages during World War II and was a significant breakthrough in computer technology.

After World War II, electronic computers began to be developed for scientific and commercial purposes. In 1945, John von Neumann developed the von Neumann architecture, which is still used in computer design today. The first commercially available computer, the UNIVAC, was introduced in 1951. It was massive and expensive, and only a few organizations could afford it.

In the 1960s, the development of the integrated circuit made it possible to create smaller and more powerful computers. This led to the development of the first mini-computers, which were smaller than mainframes but still expensive. It was not until the 1970s that the microcomputer was developed, and it was the beginning of the computer revolution.

The first microcomputer was the Altair 8800, which was introduced in 1975. It was small, affordable, and could be used by hobbyists and small businesses. The Altair was not user-friendly and did not have a keyboard or a monitor. Still, it was the beginning of the personal computer era.

In the late 1970s, Apple and IBM introduced the first personal computers. These computers were user-friendly and had a graphical user interface, which made them more accessible to the general public. The first Apple computer, the Apple II, was introduced in 1977, and the first IBM PC was introduced in 1981.

Since then, the development of computers has been rapid, and they have become smaller, faster, and more powerful. The internet, introduced in the

1990s, made it possible to connect computers worldwide, leading to the development of new applications and services. The rise of mobile devices, such as smartphones and tablets, has made computing even more accessible, and they have become an integral part of daily life.

Basic Operations of a Computer

Input, processing, output

Computers are like little robots that can understand and follow instructions to complete tasks. These tasks can range from simple things like adding numbers to more complex tasks like creating a movie or designing a website. To complete these tasks, computers use three basic operations: input, processing, and output.

Input. Input is when we give the computer information or instructions to work with. This can be by typing on the keyboard, clicking a mouse, or using a touch screen. The computer then takes this input and stores it in its memory to use later.

Processing. Once the computer has the input, it starts to process the information. This is like when you think about a problem and figure out what to do next. The computer uses a series of instructions called a program to perform specific tasks. The program tells the computer what to do with the input and how to manipulate the information to produce the desired result.

Output. The final step is the output, when the

computer produces the result of the processing. This can be in the form of a printed document, a display on the screen, or even a sound. The computer takes the processed information and presents it in a way that is easy for us to understand.

Let's take a simple example to understand the basic operations of a computer: Imagine you want to add up two numbers, 5 and 3. To do this on a computer, you would use a program or a calculator application. You would input the two numbers by typing them on the keyboard. The computer would then process the information by performing the addition. Finally, the computer would output the result, 8, either on the screen or as a printed document.

It is important to remember that computers do not think or make decisions on their own. They can only perform tasks that they have been programmed to do. The power of computers lies in their ability to perform complex calculations and process large amounts of data very quickly. This makes them incredibly useful tools for solving problems, creating new things, and storing and accessing information.

By understanding how these operations work together, we can use computers more effectively and efficiently to complete a wide range of tasks. Whether we want to do some simple math, create a website, or analyze complex data, computers are powerful tools that can help us achieve our goals.

How do computers process data and perform tasks?

As we learned in the previous section, computers use the basic operations of input, processing, and output to complete tasks. But how exactly do they process data and perform tasks?

Computers process data and perform tasks by following a series of instructions called a program or software. Programs are written in code, which is a special language that computers understand. The code tells the computer exactly what to do with the data and how to perform the task.

Programs are made up of a series of commands, each of which is a simple instruction for the computer to follow. For example, a simple program might tell the computer to:

1. Take two numbers from the user.
2. Add the two numbers together.
3. Display the result on the screen.

When the computer runs this program, it follows each command in order, starting with taking the two numbers from the user. It then adds the two numbers together and displays the result on the screen. This is a very simple example, but programs can be much more complex and involve many more commands. For example, a program that creates a movie might include instructions for the computer to:

1. Read in images and sounds.
2. Process the images and sounds to create the desired effect.
3. Put the images and sounds together in the correct order.
4. Play the movie on the screen.

Each of these commands is a simple instruction for the computer to follow. Still, when combined, they result in a much more complex and sophisticated task.

One of the key things that make computers so powerful is their ability to process and store large amounts of data very fast. They use a type of memory called RAM (Random Access Memory) to store data and perform calculations. RAM is like the computer's short-term memory, and it is used to store information that the computer is currently working with.

When the computer needs to perform a task, it reads the instructions from the program and stores the data it needs in RAM. The computer then performs the calculations and manipulates the data using the Central Processing Unit (CPU), the computer's brain. The CPU follows the instructions in the program and performs the task. Once the task is complete, the computer can store the result on the hard drive, which is the computer's long-term memory. This allows us to save the result and access it later, even after the computer has been turned off.

By understanding how computers process data and perform tasks, we can create more complex programs and use computers to their full potential to solve problems and create new things. Whether we want to add two numbers, create a movie, or analyze complex data, computers are powerful tools that can help us achieve our goals.

Types of Computers

Computers come in different shapes, sizes, and forms, each designed for a specific purpose. Whether you're using a personal computer at home, a server in a large organization, or a mobile device while you're on the go, understanding the different types of computers is important to appreciate their role in our modern world. So, let's take a closer look at the different types of computers and how they are different. In this section, we'll learn about the different types of computers, their key features, and how they are used in our daily lives.

Personal computers
Personal computers, also known as PCs, are the most common type of computer you might be familiar with. They are designed to be used by one person at a time and are great for tasks like browsing the internet, checking emails, working on documents, playing games, and much more. Personal computers come in different sizes and configurations but typically have the following components:

- A central processing unit (CPU) – this is the "brain" of the computer that processes information and performs tasks.
- Memory (RAM) – this is where the computer stores information temporarily while it is being processed.
- Storage (hard drive or solid-state drive) – this is where the computer stores information and files permanently.
- A display screen – this is what you look at to see what the computer is doing
- Keyboard and mouse – these are the most common input devices that you use to control the computer.
- Speakers – these let you hear sound from the computer.

Personal computers run on different operating systems, such as Microsoft Windows, Apple macOS, or Linux. These operating systems provide a user-friendly interface and essential tools for everyday tasks, such as creating and editing documents, connecting to the internet, and managing files.

They are highly versatile and can be used for various purposes, from work and education to entertainment and communication. They have become an essential part of our daily lives. They have significantly increased our productivity and ability to access information and connect with others. Whether you are a student, a professional, or simply someone who enjoys using technology, a personal computer is a must-have tool that can help you achieve your goals.

Servers

Servers are specialized computers designed to manage and store information and provide services to other computers and devices on a network. They play a crucial role in many organizations and businesses by supporting critical operations and applications. Some examples of the tasks that servers perform include:
- Storing and managing large amounts of data, such as customer information, financial records, and emails.
- Running websites and web-based applications.
- Hosting email and instant messaging services.
- Sharing resources, such as printers and files, with other computers on a network.

Servers are typically more powerful than personal computers. They have a more robust architecture to handle the demands of running large, complex applications and serving many users simultaneously. They may have multiple CPUs, large amounts of memory and storage, and specialized hardware components that improve performance and reliability.

One of the key differences between servers and personal computers is that servers are often configured to run 24/7, meaning they are always on and available to provide services to users. They are also typically maintained by a dedicated team of IT professionals who monitor their performance and ensure they remain secure and up-to-date.

Servers play a critical role in enabling organizations and businesses to effectively manage and share information and to provide a wide range of services and applications to users. Whether you work in an office, run a business, or use the internet, you interact with servers daily.

Mobile devices

Mobile devices, such as smartphones and tablets, are portable computers that allow us to stay connected and productive while on the go. These devices are small, lightweight, and easy to carry, making them a convenient way to access information and communicate with others from almost anywhere.

Some of the tasks that mobile devices can perform include:
- Making phone calls and sending text messages.
- Accessing the internet and browsing websites.
- Sending and receiving emails.
- Taking photos and videos.
- Running a variety of apps, such as games, social media, and productivity tools.

Mobile devices are powered by tiny, energy-efficient processors and run on batteries, allowing us to use them for several hours or even days without needing to plug them in. They also typically have touchscreens and built-in cameras, making them easy to use and providing new ways to interact with technology.

One of the biggest advantages of mobile devices is that they allow us to stay connected with friends, family, and colleagues even when we're away from our desks. Whether we're on a train, in a park, or just sitting in a coffee shop, we can use our mobile devices to stay informed, entertained, and productive.

Mobile devices are an increasingly important part of our lives, and they offer us a new way to interact with technology and stay connected with others. Whether you're looking for a way to stay productive, stay in touch with friends and family, or have fun, a mobile device is right for you!

The Computer

What are the Components of a Computer?

Computers are made up of many different parts that work together to perform tasks and store information. The most important parts of a computer include the following:
- The central processing unit (CPU).
- The random access memory (RAM).
- The hard disk drive (HDD).
- The motherboard.
- The graphics processing unit (GPU).
- The power supply unit (PSU).
- Input/output (I/O) devices.

Each computer component has a specific job, and they all work together to make the computer run smoothly. Let's look at how these parts come together to make a computer work.

Central Processing Unit (CPU)

The Central Processing Unit (CPU) is the brain of the computer. It is responsible for performing all the calculations and operations a computer needs. Think of it as the person in charge of making decisions for the computer.

The CPU is made up of two main components: the control unit and the arithmetic logic unit (ALU). The control unit retrieves instructions from memory and directs the flow of data and commands to the ALU. The ALU performs mathematical and logical operations, like adding, subtracting, comparing, and more.

When you use your computer to perform a task, like writing an email or playing a game, the CPU retrieves the instructions needed to perform that task from memory and performs the calculations. The CPU is designed to perform these calculations very quickly, allowing the computer to perform many tasks simultaneously.

In addition to performing calculations, the CPU also manages the flow of information between the different parts of the computer. It communicates with the other components, such as the RAM and the GPU, to ensure that the computer functions efficiently and effectively.

It is important to note that not all CPUs are the same. Some CPUs are designed for specific tasks, like gaming or video editing, and are optimized for those tasks. Others are designed for general use and are a good choice for most people.

Random Access Memory (RAM)

Imagine your computer is like a room in a house. Just like a room can only hold so much stuff at a time, your computer can only work with a limited amount of information at a time. That's where RAM comes in.

RAM is like a table in the room. When you're working on something, you put the things you need to remember on the table to easily access them. The table can only hold so many things at a time, just like the RAM can only store a certain amount of information.

But, unlike a table, RAM is a type of computer memory that is very fast and is used to store the data and instructions that your computer is currently working on. This way, your computer doesn't have to go back to the hard drive to get the information it needs every time t needs. Instead, it can get the information from the RAM much faster.

The more RAM you have, the more information your computer can store and work with at the same time. This means that having more RAM can make your computer run faster and more smoothly, especially if you're running multiple programs or tasks at once.

It's important to note that the information stored in RAM is only temporary. When you turn off your computer or restart it, the information stored in RAM is lost. That's why t's different from a hard drive, which is a type of long-term memory that stores your files and data even when the computer is turned off.

In a nutshell, RAM is a type of computer memory used to store the data and instructions your computer is currently working on. It's fast and helps your computer run more smoothly, but the information stored in it is only temporary.

Hard Disk Drive (HDD)

A hard disk drive, or HDD, is a crucial computer component that stores all important data and information. Imagine a library where all of your favorite books are kept. Just like a library, an HDD keeps all the important files and information you use on your computer.

An HDD is made up of a spinning disk, called a platter, inside a metal casing. The platter is divided into many tiny sections, called sectors, that can store data. A read/write head, similar to a tiny arm, floats above the disk, reading the data from and writing the data to the disk.

Think of the platter as a giant cookie platter with many little pieces of information, or "cookies," stored all over it. The read/write head is like a cookie monster that can grab one cookie at a time and move it to the computer to be used or store a new cookie on the platter.

Having an HDD in a computer is important because it provides a place to store all the information and files that the computer uses. Without an HDD, a computer couldn't save any of the work you do or the files you download.

An HDD also helps your computer run faster and more efficiently because it can access and use information faster than it would if it had to retrieve it from the internet every time you needed it.

Motherboard

The motherboard is the main circuit board in a computer and is sometimes referred to as the "heart" of the computer. Think of it like the roads and highways connecting all the different city parts. Just like roads and highways connect different parts of a city, the motherboard connects all the different computer parts together.

The motherboard is where all computer components communicate with each other and with the CPU. It's also where the CPU and other components receive power from the power supply unit.

The motherboard has slots for different components, such as the CPU, RAM, and expansion cards. These slots are like the exits and entrances of a city, where cars and trucks can drive in and out. When you add or upgrade a component, you insert it into one of these slots.

Another essential component of the motherboard is the BIOS (Basic Input/Output System). The BIOS is like the traffic cop of a city, making sure all the different parts of a computer communicate with each other properly and start-up in the right order. When you turn on your computer, the BIOS checks all the components and starts the operating system.

Graphics Processing Unit (GPU)

A Graphics Processing Unit (GPU) is a computer component responsible for creating images and animations on a computer screen. It is an essential part of a computer because it makes it possible for us to watch videos, play games, and see colorful images and animations.

Think of a GPU as an artist's paintbrush. Just as an artist uses a paintbrush to paint on a canvas and create a picture, a GPU uses its many tiny transistors to create images and animations on a computer screen. A GPU is much faster at creating these images and animations than a CPU, which is why GPUs are especially important for tasks that require a lot of graphics processing, like video games.

A GPU is like a team of artists all working together to paint a picture. Just as many artists working together can paint a picture faster than one artist working alone, many transistors working together in a GPU can create images and animations faster than a CPU.

GPUs come in many different shapes and sizes, but they all work in essentially the same way. They use many tiny transistors to process and create images and are connected to the rest of the computer by the motherboard.

Power Supply Unit (PSU)

The Power Supply Unit, also known as the PSU, is responsible for providing power to all the other components of the computer so that they can work and do their job. The PSU pumps power to all the other parts, like the CPU, RAM, GPU, and HDD.

Think of the PSU as a battery that keeps the computer running. When you turn on your computer, the PSU starts working, providing power to all the components. It also makes sure that the power it provides is steady and consistent so that the computer can run smoothly and avoid any sudden power outages or crashes.

The PSU also has a vital role in keeping the computer safe. It helps protect the computer from power surges and other power problems that could damage it. When there is a power surge, the PSU is designed to shut off the power to the computer so that it is protected from any harm.

When choosing a PSU for your computer, it is important to pick the right one for your needs. You want to make sure that it provides enough power for all the components and that it also has the safety features that you need. Some PSUs are more efficient and provide more power than others. Some are better at protecting your computer from power problems.

Input/Output (I/O) Devices

Input/Output (I/O) Devices are responsible for communicating between the computer and the outside world. These devices allow the computer to receive information from the user, such as mouse clicks and keyboard strokes and provide information back to the user, such as display images and sound. Understanding I/O devices is essential in understanding how computers work, as they allow us to interact with the computer and receive information from it.

There are many types of I/O devices, including input

devices such as keyboards, mouses, and touchpads and output devices such as displays, speakers, and printers.

Keyboards are one of the most common input devices, and they allow the user to input text and control commands into the computer. They consist of a series of buttons, each with a specific function, such as letters, numbers, and symbols. Some keyboards have additional buttons for specific functions, such as volume control or media playback.

Mouses and touchpads are other standard input devices used for pointing and clicking on objects on the computer screen. They work by moving a cursor on the screen and clicking on icons, buttons, or other objects to activate them.

Displays, such as monitors, are the primary output device of a computer. They show images, videos, and text and allow the user to see the results of their actions and the information they receive from the computer. There are different types of displays, including CRT (Cathode Ray Tube), LCD (Liquid Crystal Display), and OLED (Organic Light Emitting Diode) displays, each with its own advantages and disadvantages.

Speakers are another important output device, allowing the computer to produce sound. They work by converting electrical signals into sound waves that can be heard by the user. Many computers have built-in speakers, but external speakers can also be used for better sound quality.

Printers are used for printing text and images on

paper. There are different types of printers, including inkjet, laser, and 3D printers, each with its own advantages and disadvantages. They work by depositing nk or toner onto paper to produce a physical copy of the text, images, or other data.

Whether it's typing on a keyboard, moving a mouse, or hearing sound from speakers, these devices allow us to interact with the computer and make use of its many functions.

How does a Computer Work?

How a computer starts up?

The start-up process (the boot process) of a computer is the sequence of steps that a computer follows when it is turned on. The process starts with the press of the power button and ends with the display of the operating system (OS) on the screen. Here is a simple explanation of how the boot process works:
- Power-on: When you press the power button, the computer's power supply unit (PSU) sends electricity to all computer components. The PSU is responsible for providing power to all the components in the computer.
- BIOS Check: The Basic Input/Output System (BIOS) checks the computer's hardware to make sure everything is working correctly. The BIOS also checks to see if the computer has a bootable device connected to it, such as a hard disk drive (HDD) or a solid-state drive (SSD).
- Load Bootloader: If a bootable device is found, the BIOS will load the bootloader. The bootloader is a small program that is stored on the hard disk. Its job is to load the operating system.
- Operating System Load: The bootloader loads the operating system from the hard disk into the computer's random access memory (RAM). The operating system is now ready to start and run on

the computer.
- Initialization: The operating system performs a series of checks and initializations, such as checking the system resources and setting up the network.
- Login Screen: After the operating system has finished initializing, the login screen is displayed on the screen. The user can now enter their username and password to log into the operating system.

The boot process is a crucial step in starting up a computer. It ensures that the computer is working correctly and that the operating system is loaded and ready to use. Understanding the boot process is important for troubleshooting and fixing any problems that may occur during a computer's start-up.

It is important to note that the specific details of the boot process may vary depending on the operating system and the computer's hardware configuration. However, the basic steps are similar for most computers.

How are programs run on a computer?

Computers are capable of running various applications and programs to perform different tasks. To understand how programs are run on a computer, it's important to know a few basic terms:
- Programs are sets of instructions that tell the computer what to do. There are many different types of programs, including software applications, operating systems, and utilities.

- Applications are programs that allow you to perform specific tasks, such as word processing, email, or web browsing.
- Operating System (OS) is the software that manages the computer's hardware resources and provides services to applications. Microsoft Windows, Mac OS, and Linux are the most common operating systems.

Now that you have a basic understanding of what programs and operating systems are let's take a closer look at how programs are run on a computer.

When you click on an application icon, the operating system retrieves the program from the hard disk drive (HDD). It loads it into the computer's random access memory (RAM). The CPU then reads the program's instructions and executes them one by one.

As the program runs, the CPU retrieves data from RAM as needed, performs calculations, and writes the results back to RAM. This process continues until the program is complete or until you close it.

When the program runs, the CPU is constantly working to execute its instructions. The faster the CPU, the more instructions it can execute in a given amount of time. This is why having a fast CPU is important if you want your programs to run quickly and smoothly.

One important thing to note is that while a program runs, the CPU cannot perform any other tasks. This is why multitasking is important - it allows you to run multiple programs at the same time without having to wait for each one to finish.

Multitasking is made possible by the operating system, which manages the computer's resources and assigns CPU time to each running program. When you switch between programs, the operating system temporarily suspends one program and switches to another, allowing you to work on multiple tasks simultaneously.

How is data stored and retrieved on a computer?

Data storage and retrieval is an essential component of a computer system. It involves storing information, such as documents, photos, and music, on a computer and retrieving it when needed.

The hard disk drive (HDD) is the main component used to store data in a computer. The HDD is a spinning disk with magnetic coatings that stores the data in binary form, which is a series of 1s and 0s. The data is stored on the disk in a specific pattern corresponding to the information being stored. The HDD is like a large library, where each book is stored on a specific shelf and can be retrieved when needed.

When the computer needs to access data stored on the disk, the disk drive head moves to the location of the data, reads it, and transfers it to the computer's random access memory (RAM), where the data is temporarily stored. The data is then processed by the central processing unit (CPU), and the results are displayed on the screen or saved to the disk.

One of the most important concepts in data storage

and retrieval is the file system. A file system is a method by which data is organized on a computer's disk. There are many file systems, but the most common is the hierarchical file system. This file system organizes data into a hierarchy of folders and files, just like a traditional filing cabinet. Folders are used to organize data into related groups, and files are the individual pieces of data that make up the folders.

To store data on a computer, the user simply needs to copy or create a file in a folder. To retrieve data, the user must navigate the file system hierarchy and find the specific file they are looking for. The computer can also use indexing and search features to help the user quickly find a specific file or set of files.

Another important concept in data storage and retrieval is backup. Backup is the process of creating a copy of the data stored on a computer, usually on another disk or in the cloud, so that the data can be restored in case of a disk failure or other data loss. Regular backups are critical to protecting against data loss, as disk drives can and do fail.

The Internet

What is the Internet?

What is the Internet, and how it works?
The Internet is a global network of computers and computer networks connected to one another. It enables the sharing of information, resources, and communication worldwide. The Internet has revolutionized how we communicate, work, learn, and access information.

The Internet is made up of millions of individual computer networks and devices, such as computers, smartphones, and servers, that are connected to one another. These devices use standard communication protocols, such as the Internet Protocol (IP), to communicate with each other. When you connect your computer to the Internet, you join a network that spans the entire world.

The Internet allows for the sharing of information, resources, and communication. For example, you can use the Internet to access and share information, such as news articles, videos, and images, as well as to communicate with others through email, instant messaging, and social media. Additionally, you can use the Internet to access various services, such as online banking, online shopping, and file sharing.

The Internet is constantly evolving, with new technologies and services being developed all the time. The rise of the World Wide Web, the invention of cloud computing, and the growth of social media are just a few of the many innovations that have had a major impact on the Internet in recent years.

Whether you're using it to access information, communicate with others, or access various services, the Internet is an essential part of modern life that has transformed how we live and work.

A brief history of the Internet

The Internet has its roots in the late 1960s when the United States Department of Defense established a research project called the ARPANET. The goal of the ARPANET was to create a secure and reliable communication network that would allow researchers to share information and resources. The first ARPANET connection was established between two universities in California in 1969. Over the next several years, the network grew to include more universities and research institutions. It soon became clear that the ARPANET was an important tool for communication and collaboration.

In the 1970s, the ARPANET expanded beyond the research community and began to be used by government agencies and private companies. During this time, the Internet Protocol (IP) was developed, which is now the foundation of the Internet. IP is the underlying technology that allows data to be transmitted between computers on the network.

In the 1980s, the ARPANET was officially disbanded, and the National Science Foundation (NSF) established a new network called the NSFNET, which was designed to provide high-speed connectivity for researchers and educators. The NSFNET was the first wide-area network (WAN) to connect computers nationally and played a critical role in developing the Internet.

In the 1990s, the NSFNET was replaced by the commercial Internet, designed to provide Internet access to the general public. This was a turning point in the history of the Internet, as it allowed millions of people to access the network for the first time. The commercial Internet was based on the World Wide Web (WWW), a new way of organizing and accessing the information on the Internet. The first website was created in 1991, and the number of websites and users grew rapidly over the next few years.

In the 2000s, the Internet continued to evolve with the introduction of social media, online shopping, and other new technologies. The Internet has become an omnipresent part of everyday life, connecting people from all over the world and changing how we communicate, work, and play.

Today, the Internet is an essential tool for communication and commerce, and it continues to evolve and change at an incredible pace. The Internet has transformed how we live and work and will likely continue to shape the future in many ways that we can't yet imagine. The Internet is truly one of the greatest technological achievements of our time.

How the Internet Works?

The underlying technology that makes the Internet possible

The Internet is a massive network of interconnected computer systems that allows people to share information and communicate with each other from anywhere in the world. This network is made possible by a combination of technologies that work together to transmit and receive data across the globe.

At the heart of the Internet is a network of computers and servers connected using a standard protocol. This protocol is called Transmission Control Protocol/Internet Protocol (TCP/IP), and it provides the basic framework for transmitting data over the Internet.

When you send a message or request information from a website, your computer sends that data to a server. This server, in turn, sends the data to other servers until it reaches its final destination. Each server in the network acts as a relay, forwarding the data to the next server in the network until it reaches its final destination.

The data transmitted over the Internet is broken down into small packets. Each packet contains a portion of the data and is sent independently to its destination. The recipient computer then reassembles the packets to form the complete message or information.

This process of breaking down data into packets and transmitting it across the Internet is known as packet switching. Packet switching allows the Internet to transmit large amounts of data quickly and efficiently, and it is the key technology that makes the Internet possible.

To transmit data over long distances, the Internet uses a system of interconnected networks known as routers. Routers are specialized computers that connect different parts of the Internet and route data between them. They use complex algorithms to determine the most efficient path for data to travel, and they help to ensure that data reaches its final destination as quickly and reliably as possible.

In addition to packet switching and routers, the Internet relies on high-speed communication links, such as fiber optic cables and satellite connections, to transmit data at high speeds. These communication links are responsible for transmitting the vast amounts of data sent over the Internet daily.

How data travels across the Internet?

When we access the Internet, we send and receive data from other computers on the network. The underlying technology that makes this possible is "packet switching."

Each packet is sent to its destination via a series of routers. Routers are the devices that direct traffic on the Internet. They are responsible for deciding which route each packet should take to reach its destination. The route a packet takes is determined by several factors, including the speed and availability of different network paths.

When a packet arrives at a router, the router reads the destination address and decides which route to send the packet next. The router then sends the packet to its next destination, where it is again examined and sent on to the next router, and so on, until the packet reaches its final destination.

As the packets are transmitted across the Internet, they may encounter delays or congestion. If this happens, some packets may be delayed or even lost. To ensure that the data is transmitted reliably, the Internet uses a protocol called Transmission Control Protocol (TCP).

TCP is responsible for detecting lost or delayed packets and retransmitting them if necessary. This ensures that all the packets arrive at their destination and are reassembled into the original data in the correct order.

Common Internet Services

The Internet is a vast network of connected devices and servers that allows us to access and share information with people around the world. It has evolved significantly since its inception and now offers users a wide range of services. Let's talk about the most common Internet services.

Web Browsers

Web browsers are software applications that allow users to access and view the content of the Internet. A web browser communicates with servers on the Internet, retrieves the content of websites, and displays it to the user. Web browsers are essential for accessing the vast wealth of information available on the Internet and for conducting online activities such as online shopping, online banking, and social media.

The first web browser, called WorldWideWeb, was developed by Sir Tim Berners-Lee in 1990. Since then, many web browsers have been developed and are now widely used, including Google Chrome, Mozilla Firefox, Microsoft Edge, and Apple's Safari. These web browsers differ in terms of their design, functionality, and features they offer. Still, they all serve the same primary purpose of providing access to the Internet.

When using a web browser, you can navigate to websites by entering the URL or web address of the website into the address bar. The browser then sends a request to the server that hosts the website, asking for the content of the website. The server sends back the content, which the browser displays on your computer.

The content of a website is typically written in a markup language, such as HTML or XHTML, and may also use other technologies, such as JavaScript, Cascading Style Sheets (CSS), and multimedia content, like images and videos. The web browser uses these technologies to render the content of the website and display it in a visually appealing way.

Besides displaying web pages, web browsers offer many other features, such as bookmarks, history, and tabs. Bookmarks allow you to save the addresses of your favorite websites for quick access in the future. The history feature lets you view the websites you have visited recently. Tabs allow you to open multiple websites at the same time in the same browser window, making it easier to switch between them.

Web browsers also offer security features, such as blocking pop-up ads and protection against malicious websites. Some web browsers also offer private browsing mode, which does not store the history of your online activities, and incognito mode, which does not store any data about your online activities, including cookies and temporary internet files.

Web browsers are an essential tool for accessing the Internet and its vast wealth of information. Whether you're shopping, banking, or simply browsing the web, a web browser provides an easy and convenient way to connect to the Internet and take advantage of its many services.

Email

The email is a widely used service on the Internet that allows users to send and receive messages and attachments electronically. The term "email" is short for "electronic mail." This service was first introduced in the 1960s and has since become one of the most important communication tools in the digital age.

The way email works is simple. When a user sends an email, the message is sent from their computer to an email server. The email server then sends the message to the recipient's email server. The recipient's email server then delivers the message to the recipient's email client application, such as Microsoft Outlook or Gmail.

An email address is required to send and receive emails. An email address is a unique identifier assigned to a person or an organization. It usually consists of a combination of a username and a domain name, such as "username@example.com."

Emails can be sent and received from anywhere in the world as long as there is an internet connection. This makes email a convenient way for people to communicate with each other regardless of where they are located.

In addition to sending text messages, emails can include attachments such as images, videos, and documents. This makes email a versatile communication tool that can be used for various purposes, including personal and professional communication, sending job applications and more.

Another benefit of email is that it is relatively secure. Email providers have implemented various security measures to prevent unauthorized access to email accounts. But we will discuss security in the next chapter about Security on the Internet.

File sharing

File sharing refers to distributing or providing access to digital information, such as computer programs, multimedia (audio, images, and video), documents, and electronic books. File sharing allows users to share their files with others over the Internet.

File sharing is possible through various means, including peer-to-peer (P2P) networks, cloud storage services, and online file-sharing platforms. Peer-to-peer networks allow users to connect directly to each other and exchange files. In P2P file sharing, files are transferred directly from one user's device to another's without passing through a central server.

Cloud storage services are online platforms that allow users to store their data on remote servers. With cloud storage, users can access their files from anywhere and at any time, as long as they have an Internet connection. Some popular cloud storage services include Google Drive, Apple iCloud, and Dropbox.

Online file-sharing platforms provide a platform for users to share their files with others. These platforms usually require users to create an account to use the service and allow them to upload and share their files with other users. Some popular online file-sharing platforms include WeTransfer, Hightail, and MediaFire.

File sharing is a convenient and efficient way to exchange information and collaborate with others. It allows users to share large files quickly and easily without relying on physical media, such as USB drives or external hard drives. Additionally, file sharing can help reduce costs, eliminating the need for expensive storage devices or data transfer methods.

Social media

Social media refers to websites and applications that allow users to share and create content, as well as participate in virtual communities and networks. Some of the most popular social media platforms include Facebook, Instagram, Twitter, TikTok, and LinkedIn. Social media platforms provide a space for users to connect with friends, family, and other people with similar interests and share news, ideas, photos, and videos.

One of the most significant advantages of social media is the ability to connect with people from all over the world, regardless of distance or location. Social media has changed how people communicate and has made it easier to stay in touch with friends and family. Additionally, social media platforms can be used to stay informed about current events or to promote a business or product.

However, social media can also have negative effects. For example, excessive use of social media has been linked to increased anxiety and depression, as well as decreased self-esteem. Furthermore, social media has been criticized for spreading false information and promoting negative or harmful content.

Despite these potential downsides, social media

remains an integral part of modern society and continues to be one of the most widely used internet services. If used in moderation and with caution, social media can be a valuable tool for staying connected, learning new information, and promoting positive change.

Online shopping

Online shopping refers to purchasing products or services through the Internet. This method of shopping has become increasingly popular in recent years due to the convenience and accessibility it offers. With just a few clicks, people can buy almost anything from anywhere in the world and have it delivered to their doorsteps.

Online shopping allows consumers to compare prices, products, and services offered by different vendors and retailers, making it easier for them to find the best deals. This is because most online stores have a vast range of products and services, and customers can easily browse through them to find what they need. Additionally, online shopping can be done anywhere, whether in the comfort of your home or on the go with a mobile device.

One of the biggest benefits of online shopping is the convenience it offers. There is no need to physically visit stores and waste time searching for products. All you need is a computer or mobile device and an internet connection. Customers can easily search for products, compare prices, and make purchases with just a few clicks. Online shopping also eliminates the need to wait in line to make a purchase, which can be time-consuming and frustrating.

Another advantage of online shopping is the ability to purchase products from anywhere in the world. This has opened up a new world of opportunities for both consumers and businesses. Customers can now purchase products from international retailers and have them delivered to their doorstep, making it easier for them to access a wider range of products and services.

Online shopping has revolutionized the way people purchase products and services. With its convenience, accessibility, and wide range of options, it's no wonder why it has become so popular in recent years. If you haven't tried online shopping yet, it's definitely worth exploring and discovering the benefits it has to offer.

Online banking

Online banking is a service that allows you to manage your financial transactions and activities through the Internet. This service provides a convenient and secure way to access your bank account information and perform banking transactions from anywhere, as long as you have an

Internet connection.

Online banking lets you view your account balances and transactions, transfer funds between accounts, pay bills and even deposit checks. You can also access investment and financial planning tools and receive electronic statements and other important information.

To use online banking, you must first have an account with a bank or credit union that offers the service. Once you have an account, you can log in to the bank's website using your username and password. From there, you will be able to access all of the online banking services that the bank provides.

One of the key benefits of online banking is that it is typically more convenient than traditional banking methods. You can perform transactions 24 hours a day, 7 days a week, without visiting a physical bank branch. This is especially helpful if you live in a remote location or your schedule doesn't allow you to visit a bank during regular business hours.

Another advantage of online banking is that it is generally more secure than traditional banking methods. Banks use encryption and other security measures to protect your personal and financial information. They often monitor transactions for suspicious activity to prevent fraud.

Despite its many benefits, there are some risks

associated with online banking. For example, your personal and financial information may be at risk if you use an unsecured or public Wi-Fi connection, click on a malicious link, or download a malicious file. To protect yourself, it's important to use a secure and trusted internet connection, to keep your passwords and other sensitive information confidential, and to always be cautious when providing personal or financial information online.

Now that you've seen how important it is to stay safe online, it's time to dig deeper into Security on the Internet.

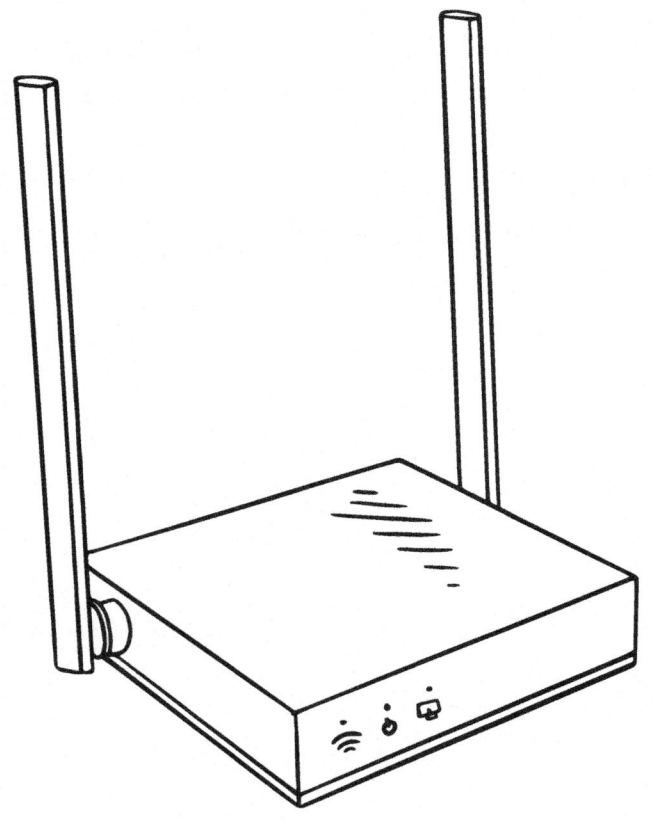

Security on the Internet

What is Internet Security?

The Internet is a vast and complex network that has become an integral part of our daily lives. With its widespread use comes the need for security to protect ourselves and our sensitive information from cyber threats. Internet security is the practice of protecting computer systems and networks from unauthorized access, use, disclosure, disruption, modification, or destruction.

Internet security is crucial for many reasons. The Internet is a vast and open network, which makes it vulnerable to cyber attacks, such as viruses, malware, and other forms of cybercrime. The more sensitive the data, the more important it is to protect it from potential cyber threats. Internet security is essential for businesses, governments, and individuals who use the Internet to conduct their operations or store sensitive information.

There are many types of security threats on the Internet, including phishing attacks, viruses, malware, ransomware, spyware, and social engineering attacks. Phishing attacks occur when cybercriminals attempt to steal sensitive information, such as login credentials or credit card information, by sending fake emails or messages that appear to be from a legitimate source. Viruses, malware, ransomware, and spyware are malicious software programs that infect a computer system or network and can cause damage or steal sensitive information. Social engineering attacks are when attackers manipulate people into divulging sensitive information, usually by pretending to be someone else or offering something that seems too good to be true.

Internet security is constantly evolving, and in today's digital age, it has become an increasingly critical issue as more and more personal information is being transmitted over the Internet. As a result, internet security is now an essential aspect of our daily lives, and it involves protecting information from unauthorized access, theft, and other malicious activities.

Why is Internet Security Important?

Personal privacy

One of the most significant reasons to protect your internet security is to maintain your personal privacy. When you access the Internet, you leave a digital trail that can be traced back to your location, identity, and browsing history. This information can be used by cybercriminals to steal your identity or even used by advertisers to track your online behavior.

Protection of financial information

The Internet is used for a wide range of financial transactions, including online banking, e-commerce, and other money transfer services. Therefore, internet security is crucial in protecting your sensitive financial information from unauthorized access and theft.

Preventing cybercrime

The Internet is home to numerous cyber threats, including phishing scams, malware, viruses, and other malicious attacks. Cyber-attacks can lead to identity theft, data breaches, and financial loss.

Internet security measures are critical in protecting you from these threats.

Protecting against data breaches

Data breaches occur when cybercriminals gain unauthorized access to sensitive information such as credit card details, passwords, and other confidential information. Such breaches can result in massive financial loss and even legal action. Internet security measures such as encryption, two-factor authentication, and other technologies can help protect against data breaches.

Maintaining business reputation

Organizations can also suffer from poor internet security practices. Data breaches can damage an organization's reputation, leading to loss of business and revenue. Therefore, businesses must take internet security seriously to protect their customers' personal information.

The importance of internet security cannot be overemphasized. With the increasing number of cyber threats, protecting your personal information and financial data is vital. Internet security measures such as passwords, firewalls, antivirus software, and encryption are necessary to protect against cybercrime and prevent data breaches.

Different Types of Security Threats on the Internet

The Internet has revolutionized how we communicate, work, and live. However, this technological advancement has brought about a new set of security challenges that we must all be aware of. Cybersecurity threats are constantly evolving, and it is crucial to understand the different types of security threats that exist to take appropriate measures to protect ourselves and our information.
- Malware: Malware is any software designed to damage, disrupt, or gain unauthorized access to a computer system. Examples of malware include viruses, worms, Trojans, and ransomware. Malware can be spread through emails, file-sharing networks, and other means.
- Phishing: Phishing is a type of social engineering attack that involves tricking users into providing sensitive information, such as usernames, passwords, and credit card numbers. Phishing attacks are often delivered through emails, text messages, or phone calls that appear to be from legitimate sources, such as banks, social media

platforms, or e-commerce websites.
- Denial of Service (DoS) Attacks: A DoS attack is when a hacker attempts to overwhelm a server, website, or network with traffic, making it unusable. This is typically achieved by flooding the target with an overwhelming number of requests, making it impossible for legitimate traffic to get through.
- Man-in-the-Middle (MitM) Attacks: A MitM attack is when a hacker intercepts the communication between two parties and eavesdrops or manipulates the communication. For example, a hacker could intercept the communication between a user and a website and then steal the user's login credentials.
- Password Attacks: Password attacks are a type of attack where a hacker attempts to guess or steal a user's password. This can be done through brute force attacks, where a hacker tries a large number of possible passwords until the correct one is found, or through social engineering attacks that trick users into revealing their passwords.
- Physical Security Threats: Physical security threats refer to any type of threat that involves physical access to computer systems or data. For example, theft or loss of laptops, smartphones, or other devices can lead to data breaches.

It is important to be aware of these types of security threats so that you can take appropriate measures to protect yourself and your information. This can include using antivirus software, enabling two-factor authertication, being careful with your passwords, and being vigilant for phishing scams. By taking steps to protect your online identity, you can ensure that your online experience is as safe and secure as possible.

Protecting Yourself Online

In the previous section, we talked about the dangers that you face on the Internet. Now, let's see what you can do to protect yourself from those threats. Here are some ways you can protect yourself online:

Passwords

Passwords are one of the most important tools you have for protecting your online accounts. A password is a combination of letters, numbers, and symbols that you use to prove your identity and gain access to your account. It is essential to choose a strong password and to change it regularly to ensure that your account is protected from unauthorized access.

To create a strong password, you should choose a combination of letters, numbers, and symbols that are not easy to guess. Avoid using easily guessable information such as your name, birthday, or favorite sports team. It is also important to use a different password for each account to ensure that a single security breach doesn't compromise all of your accounts. Avoid using easy-to-guess phrases such as "password" or "123456."

It is also important to keep your passwords secure. Don't share your passwords with anyone, and avoid writing them down or storing them in a place where they could be easily discovered. Consider using a password manager to securely store your passwords and generate strong, unique passwords for each of your accounts.

Firewalls

A firewall is a software or hardware device that acts as a barrier between a computer or network and the Internet, blocking unauthorized access to or from the computer or network while allowing authorized access. It can help prevent unauthorized access to your computer or network by monitoring and controlling the traffic between them and the Internet.

Firewalls can be configured to block traffic from specific IP addresses or applications or set to allow traffic only from specific IP addresses or applications. They can also be set to block certain types of traffic, such as email attachments or instant messaging, or to block traffic from specific ports.

Firewalls use a set of rules to determine which traffic is allowed to pass through and which is blocked. These rules can be customized to meet the specific needs of a user or network. For example, a business might set up a firewall to block access to social media sites during work hours to help keep employees focused on their tasks.

In addition to using a firewall, it's also important to keep it up to date with the latest software updates and patches. This will help ensure that the firewall can effectively block the latest threats.

Firewalls are a critical component of internet security. They can help protect you from various threats, including viruses, malware, and hackers. By understanding how they work and how to properly configure them, you can help ensure that your computer and network stay safe and secure.

Antivirus Software

Antivirus software is a program designed to prevent, detect, and remove malware from a computer or network. Malware is malicious software, such as viruses, Trojans, spyware, and ransomware, that can infect a computer and cause harm to the user.

Antivirus software works by scanning files and programs on a computer or network for signs of malware. When a virus is detected, the software will either delete the infected file or attempt to repair it. Antivirus software may also use heuristic analysis, which looks for unusual behavior in software that may be a sign of malware.

Antivirus software is vital for protecting against cyberattacks and the theft of personal information.

It is particularly important for businesses and organizations, which often have sensitive data that is valuable to cybercriminals. Antivirus software can prevent the spread of malware in a network, reducing the risk of a data breach or other security incident.

There are many antivirus software options available on the market, including both free and paid versions. When choosing an antivirus program, it is important to consider its effectiveness, ease of use, and compatibility with your operating system.

In addition to using antivirus software, other steps can be taken to protect against malware. For example, users should be cautious when downloading files or clicking on links from unknown sources. It is also important to keep software up to date, as updates often include security patches that address vulnerabilities in the software. Finally, regular backups of important data can help prevent data loss in the event of a malware attack.

Encryption

Encryption is an essential security measure for protecting your online communications. It is a key tool for staying safe on the Internet. Encryption is the process of encoding a message or data so that it can only be read by the intended recipient.

When you use encryption, your data is transformed into an unreadable format that can only be decoded by the person who has the encryption key. This makes it extremely difficult for hackers or malicious actors to intercept and read your data.

There are different types of encryption available, including symmetric and asymmetric encryption. Symmetric encryption uses the same key for both encryption and decryption. In contrast, asymmetric encryption uses two different keys - a public key and a private key. The public key is used to encrypt data, while the private key is used to decrypt it.

Many online services, such as email and messaging apps, use encryption to protect your data from interception by third parties. For example, popular email services like Gmail and Outlook use Transport Layer Security (TLS) encryption to protect email messages while in transit.

It's important to note, however, that encryption is not foolproof. While it provides an additional layer of protection, there are still ways for determined hackers to intercept and read encrypted data. It's important to use encryption and other security measures, such as strong passwords and two-factor authentication, to ensure your online safety.

There are different levels of encryption available, and not all encryption is created equal. It's important to choose services that use strong encryption algorithms and keep up-to-date with the latest security protocols to ensure your data is as secure as possible.

Two Factor Authentication

Two-Factor Authentication (2FA) is a security measure used to protect online accounts. In addition to a password, 2FA requires a second form of authentication, typically something the user has, such as a physical token, or something the user is, such as a fingerprint or facial recognition.

2FA effectively prevents unauthorized access to your online accounts, as it adds an extra layer of protection beyond a simple password. Even if an attacker were to obtain your password, they would still need the second form of authentication to access your account.

There are different types of 2FA available, but the most commonly used methods include the following:

- SMS verification: This method sends a code to your phone via text message. You enter this code to verify your identity.
- Authentication apps: There are several authenticator apps available, such as Google Authenticator or Microsoft Authenticator, which generate one-time codes that you enter to verify your identity.
- Physical security keys: A physical key that you insert into your computer or mobile device. When you log in, you press a button on the key to verify your identity.

When setting up 2FA, it's important to make sure you have a backup method in case you lose your primary form of authentication. Many services offer backup codes or the option to add a secondary phone number.

It's worth noting that while 2FA is an effective security measure, it's not foolproof. Some attacks, such as SIM swapping or phishing attacks, can bypass 2FA. However, 2FA still significantly reduces the risk of unauthorized access to your accounts.

Blockchain

What is Blockchain?

Blockchain is like a special notebook that lots of people share. Instead of just one person owning the notebook, many people have their own copy. Every time someone writes something in their notebook, everyone else who has a copy writes the same thing in their notebook too.

Now, imagine that everyone who has a copy of the notebook has to agree on what's written in it. If someone tries to change something, everyone else will notice and disagree. That's because the notebook uses mathematical computations, making it really hard to cheat or make changes without everyone else noticing.

This notebook keeps track of things like money or who owns what. Whenever someone wants to buy or sell something, they write down what they're doing in their notebook, and everyone else writes it in their own notebook too. This means that everyone knows exactly what's happening with the money or the thing being bought or sold.

And because the notebook is so secure, people can trust that the information in it is accurate. They don't have to worry about someone cheating or stealing because everyone else is watching to make sure that doesn't happen.

That's basically what Blockchain is – a special kind of notebook that many people share and use to keep track of things like money or ownership. It's secure because everyone has a copy and has to agree on what's in it. And that's what makes it so useful for online transactions and record-keeping.

How is Blockchain Used for transactions and data storage?

Blockchain is like a big book that stores information. But unlike a regular book, this can't be changed once you write something. Each time something is added to the book, it creates a new page connected to the previous one, like a chain.

People use Blockchain to keep track of things they don't want to lose or have someone else change. For example, you might want to make sure that no one can take away your money after you've earned it or change something important you've written.

One way that people use Blockchain is for transactions, which means when you buy or sell something. Think of it like buying a toy from a store. You give the store your money, and they give you the toy. The store keeps track of how much money they get from everyone and what toys they give away. They might use a computer program or a piece of paper to do this.

With Blockchain, people can keep track of transactions without needing a person or a company to do it for them. When you buy something using Blockchain, you tell the book what you want to buy and how much you want to pay for it. The book writes this down on a new page, and everyone who uses the book can see it.

But the book doesn't just write down your information. It also checks to ensure that you have the money you say you do. This is done by lots of computers all around the world that work together. They check to make sure that you aren't trying to cheat the system and that you aren't buying something you can't afford.

Once the book has checked everything, it writes down the new transaction on a new page in the book. This page is connected to the previous one, so you can see all the transactions that have happened before. This means that no one can change what happened in the past, and everyone can see what has happened.

Another way that people use Blockchain is for data storage, which means keeping track of information. Think of it like writing a letter to your friend. You might write it on paper and give it to them. Or you might send an email. Either way, you want to make sure that the information doesn't get lost or changed.

With Blockchain, people can keep track of important information without needing a person or a company to do it for them. When you write something in the book, everyone who uses the book can see it. But like before, the book checks to make sure that the information is true and hasn't been changed.

Once the book has checked everything, it writes down the new information on a new page in the book. This page is connected to the previous one, so you can see all the information written before. This means that no one can change what happened in the past, and everyone can see what has happened.

Benefits of Blockchain

Blockchain is a new technology that has the potential to revolutionize the way we do things online. It has many advantages over traditional methods of storing and sharing data, making it an important technology for the future. Here are some of the main benefits of using Blockchain.

Security
Blockchain is incredibly secure because of the way it works. Instead of relying on a single central authority to keep records, Blockchain uses a network of computers to verify transactions and store data. It is much more difficult for hackers to manipulate or steal data.

Transparency
Another advantage of Blockchain is that it is incredibly transparent. Every transaction on the Blockchain is recorded in a public ledger, so anyone can see it. This means there is no need for intermediaries to verify transactions, as the Blockchain can verify them.

Efficiency

Blockchain is also incredibly efficient. Because it is a decentralized system, transactions can be completed quickly and without the need for intermediaries. This means there is less time and money wasted on middlemen, and transactions can be completed faster.

Decentralization

Blockchain is a decentralized system, meaning there is no single point of failure. This makes it incredibly resistant to censorship, as there is no way for a single person or organization to control the network. This makes Blockchain ideal for use in situations where censorship or government control is a concern.

Trust

Another advantage of Blockchain is that it is incredibly trustworthy. Because every transaction is verified by a network of computers, there is no need to rely on third parties to verify transactions. This makes it much easier to trust the people or organizations you are dealing with and reduces the risk of fraud or other types of abuse.

Blockchain is an incredibly powerful technology that has the potential to change the way we do things online. As the technology continues to evolve and improve, we can expect to see even more innovative uses for Blockchain in the years to come.

Real-World Applications of Blockchain

Blockchain technology has been adopted by many industries and organizations for various purposes. This section will explain the different types of industries and organizations that are using Blockchain technology and how they are utilizing it.

Finance

The finance industry was one of the first to adopt Blockchain technology. Blockchain is used for a number of purposes in finance, including improving transaction speed, reducing fraud, and increasing transparency. Banks and financial institutions use Blockchain to create a more efficient and secure financial system. For example, Blockchain can settle securities transactions in real time instead of taking several days to complete.

Healthcare

The healthcare industry has also started to use Blockchain technology to improve the security and accuracy of patient records. Blockchain allows medical records to be stored securely and accessed quickly by authorized individuals. This helps to reduce medical errors and improve patient outcomes.

Supply chain management

Blockchain is being used to improve supply chain management in manufacturing, food production, and retail industries. By using Blockchain, companies can track products from the manufacturer to the end user, ensuring that they are authentic and have not been tampered with. This can help reduce waste and fraud and ensure that products are delivered to the right people at the right time.

Government

Governments around the world are exploring the use of Blockchain technology for a variety of purposes, such as voting, identity verification, and secure data storage. Blockchain can help ensure the integrity of elections by making it more difficult to manipulate voting results. It can also help governments create secure and tamper-proof identity verification systems, which can help reduce fraud and protect citizens' personal information.

Real estate

Blockchain technology can be used in real estate transactions to create a more efficient and secure system. For example, Blockchain can be used to store property records, making verifying ownership easier and reducing the risk of fraud. It can also facilitate real estate transactions, reducing the need for intermediaries and saving time and money.

Energy

Energy is another industry exploring using Blockchain technology to improve the efficiency and security of energy transactions. Blockchain can be used to track energy production and distribution, making it easier to manage the grid and reduce waste. It can facilitate peer-to-peer energy transactions, allowing individuals to buy and sell excess energy directly to one another.

Blockchain technology has the potential to revolutionize a wide range of industries by increasing transparency, improving security, and reducing inefficiencies. As the technology continues to develop, we will likely see more and more industries and organizations adopting Blockchain to help them achieve their goals.

Artificial Intelligence

What is Artificial Intelligence?

Artificial Intelligence, or AI for short, is a technology that allows machines to learn and make decisions as humans do. It is a way for computers to recognize patterns in data and use that information to make predictions or perform tasks.

AI works by using algorithms, or sets of rules, to process data and find patterns. These algorithms are designed to learn and improve over time, becoming more accurate as they are exposed to more data. The process of learning and improving is called machine learning, which is a subset of AI.

AI can be categorized into three main types: supervised learning, unsupervised learning, and reinforcement learning.

- Supervised learning is when the algorithm is trained on a labeled dataset, which means the data is already categorized or labeled.
- Unsupervised learning is when the algorithm is not given labeled data and has to find patterns and group the data on its own.

- Reinforcement learning is when the algorithm learns through trial and error by receiving feedback on its actions.

There are many ways that AI can be used to benefit society. Here are some examples of what it could do:

- Analyze medical images and help doctors make more accurate diagnoses.
- Improve customer service by using chatbots to answer questions and solve customer problems.
- Analyze stock prices and predict future trends in finance.
- Optimize processes and reduce waste.

AI can analyze large amounts of data much faster than humans and make more accurate predictions. This way, it reduces human error, as it is not subject to the same biases and inconsistencies as humans.

AI has the potential to revolutionize many aspects of society, from healthcare to finance to customer service. As technology improves, AI will likely become even more present in our lives. However, it is important to consider AI's ethical and social implications and ensure that it is used responsibly.

A brief history of AI

Artificial Intelligence (AI) is a rapidly growing field transforming how we live and work. It is a broad term used to describe machines that can perform tasks that usually require human intelligence, such as learning, problem-solving, and decision-making.

The history of AI dates back to the mid-20th century when computer scientists began to explore the possibility of creating machines that could mimic human intelligence. The term "artificial intelligence" was first coined in 1956 by John McCarthy, widely regarded as one of the field's founders.

The early years of AI research focused on developing algorithms and techniques for solving specific problems, such as playing chess or proving mathematical theorems. However, progress was slow due to the limited computing power of the time and the lack of data to train the algorithms.

In the 1980s, a technique called "expert systems" became popular, which allowed computers to make decisions based on a set of rules and knowledge provided by human experts. This led to the development of various practical applications, such as medical diagnosis and financial analysis.

The 1990s saw the emergence of machine learning, which involves training algorithms to recognize patterns and make predictions based on large amounts of data. This led to breakthroughs in areas such as speech recognition and image classification and laid the foundation for the development of modern AI.

Since then, the field of AI has exploded, with advances in deep learning, natural language processing, and robotics, among other areas. Today, AI is being used in a wide range of industries, from healthcare and finance to manufacturing and customer service.

Despite the rapid progress in AI, there are still many challenges, such as improving the accuracy and reliability of algorithms, addressing ethical and social issues, and ensuring that AI is used for the benefit of all people. As technology evolves, AI will likely play an increasingly important role in our lives, transforming our lives and work in ways we cannot yet imagine.

Types of Artificial Intelligence

Artificial intelligence (AI) is a broad field that encompasses many different approaches and techniques, each with its own strengths and weaknesses. Here are some of the most common types of AI.

Rule-Based AI
This is the simplest form of AI, where a set of rules is defined that can be used to determine an output based on a given input. For example, a rule-based AI system might be used to diagnose a medical condition based on a set of symptoms. If the patient has symptoms A, B, and C, the AI system will diagnose the condition as X.

Machine Learning
Machine learning is a form of AI that uses statistical algorithms to enable computers to learn from data. The computer is not explicitly programmed to solve a specific problem but rather learns to do so by analyzing data. For example, a machine learning system might be trained on a set of images and then used to automatically classify new images as

belonging to a particular category (e.g., dog, cat, or bird).

Natural Language Processing (NLP)

NLP is a type of AI that deals with the interaction between computers and human language. This includes speech recognition, language translation, and sentiment analysis. NLP enables chatbots and virtual assistants to understand and respond to natural language queries. The most popular example that you might already know is ChatGPT.

Neural Networks

Neural networks are a type of machine learning algorithm inspired by the human brain's structure and function. A neural network is composed of a large number of interconnected nodes, or "neurons," that work together to solve a specific problem. Neural networks are often used for image and speech recognition.

Fuzzy Logic

Fuzzy logic is a type of AI that deals with reasoning that is approximate rather than precise. Fuzzy logic is used to model and control systems that are inherently imprecise, such as air conditioning systems and traffic control systems.

Evolutionary Computation

Evolutionary computation is a type of AI that uses

algorithms inspired by biological evolution to solve problems. These algorithms start with a population of potential solutions and then "evolve" these solutions over many generations until a satisfactory solution is found.

Each type of AI has its own strengths and weaknesses, and different types are suited to different applications. By combining different types of AI, developers can create complex systems capable of solving a wide range of problems.

Benefits of Artificial Intelligence

AI systems are designed to mimic human cognitive processes such as learning, reasoning, and decision-making. The benefits of using AI are vast and varied; the first one we will explore is efficiency.

Efficiency

AI can improve efficiency in several ways. One of the most significant ways is by automating routine and repetitive tasks. This is particularly useful in industries that require a lot of data processing, such as finance, manufacturing, and healthcare. AI systems can perform these tasks much faster and more accurately than humans, freeing up time for more complex and creative work.

Another way that AI improves efficiency is by optimizing processes. AI systems can analyze data and identify patterns and anomalies that might be difficult for humans to detect. This helps businesses identify areas where they can improve processes, reduce waste, and increase productivity.

AI also improves efficiency by enabling better decision-making. AI systems can analyze large amounts of data and provide insights to help organizations make informed decisions. This is particularly useful in industries such as finance, where decisions need to be made quickly and based on a vast amount of data.

In healthcare, AI improves efficiency by helping doctors and nurses make better and faster diagnoses. AI systems can analyze medical data and provide insights to help healthcare professionals make more accurate diagnoses and develop better treatment plans.

Accuracy

One of the biggest advantages of using artificial intelligence (AI) is the potential for improved accuracy in tasks that require precision and attention to detail. AI has the ability to analyze vast amounts of data and identify patterns or anomalies that may not be noticeable to the human eye.

For example, in the medical field, AI can analyze medical images such as X-rays or MRIs to identify potential health issues or anomalies that may be difficult for a human radiologist to detect. This could lead to earlier and more accurate diagnoses, ultimately saving lives.

In finance, AI analyzes large amounts of financial data and identifies potential fraud or irregularities. This helps financial institutions identify and prevent fraudulent activities, leading to a more secure and reliable financial system.

Another example is in manufacturing, where AI monitors production lines and identifies potential quality issues or defects. This leads to improved product quality and increases customer satisfaction.

The improved accuracy provided by AI has the potential to greatly benefit various industries and applications. However, it's important to note that AI is not infallible and may still make errors or be influenced by biased data. It's important to continually monitor and refine AI systems to ensure accuracy and avoid potential negative consequences.

Decision-making

Artificial intelligence (AI) has the potential to revolutionize decision-making in various industries, making it faster, more accurate, and more data-driven. Here are some ways AI can help with decision-making:

- **Identifying patterns and trends.** AI can also identify patterns and trends in data that might be too complex for humans to discern. For example, in finance, AI can analyze financial market trends and identify patterns in stock prices, which can help investors make more informed decisions about where to invest their money.

- Real-time decision-making. In some industries, decisions must be made quickly and in real-time. For example, in the field of autonomous vehicles, AI is used to make real-time decisions about braking, accelerating, and steering based on real-time data from the vehicle's sensors. This can help improve safety and prevent accidents.
- Reduced bias: AI helps to reduce human bias in decision-making by using objective criteria to make decisions. For example, in hiring, AI algorithms can analyze resumes and job applications to identify the best candidates based on objective criteria such as skills and experience rather than factors like race, gender, or age.

Personalization

Artificial Intelligence (AI) has the ability to personalize the experiences of users, which is another important benefit. This means that it can provide personalized recommendations, tailored advertising, and customized experiences to users.

For example, when you log in to an online shopping website, the website may recommend products based on your search and purchase history. The website may also show you similar items that you might be interested in based on your past behavior. This is made possible through AI algorithms that analyze your data to provide tailored recommendations.

In healthcare, AI could help personalize treatment plans based on individual patient data. It can analyze a patient's medical history, genetic makeup, and lifestyle to create a personalized treatment plan that considers their specific needs and preferences. This leads to more effective treatment and better health outcomes for patients.

In the entertainment industry, AI helps personalize users' viewing experience. Streaming services analyze a user's watch history and recommend shows and movies they are likely to enjoy. This can keep users engaged with the platform and increase user satisfaction.

Improved Safety

Artificial Intelligence (AI) is a powerful tool that can improve safety in many applications. By analyzing data and patterns, AI can help predict potential safety risks, prevent accidents, and improve emergency response. Here are some examples of how AI can enhance safety:

Transportation. In the transportation industry, AI analyzes data and identifies potential safety risks on the road. For example, AI-powered sensors can monitor the health of vehicles in real-time, detecting any signs of wear or malfunction before an accident occurs. Autonomous vehicles, which use AI to navigate and make decisions, can also help reduce the number of accidents caused by human error.

Healthcare. In healthcare, AI identifies potential safety risks for patients. By analyzing data from electronic medical records and other sources, AI algorithms can help identify patients at risk of developing complications, such as infections or blood clots. AI can also help detect adverse drug interactions or flag potential diagnosis errors.

Manufacturing. In manufacturing, AI helps ensure the safety of workers by monitoring equipment and identifying potential hazards. For example, AI-powered sensors can detect temperature or pressure changes, indicating potential malfunctions or safety hazards.

Emergency response. In emergency response situations, AI could help improve response times and save lives. For example, AI algorithms can analyze social media and other sources to identify potential emergency situations, such as natural disasters or accidents. AI-powered drones could also be used to survey disaster areas and locate survivors.

In all these applications, AI can help enhance safety by identifying potential risks and improving response times. However, it is important to note that AI is not a silver bullet and must be used responsibly. As with any technology, potential risks and unintended consequences must be addressed.

Real-World Applications of Artificial Intelligence

Artificial Intelligence (AI) has already transformed many industries and organizations. Here are some examples of the various industries and organizations using AI.

Healthcare

Artificial Intelligence (AI) is becoming increasingly common in the healthcare industry, offering solutions to complex problems that are difficult for humans to tackle alone. By leveraging AI technology, healthcare professionals can provide more accurate diagnoses, identify potential risks, and personalize treatment plans.

One of the most promising areas for AI in healthcare is medical imaging. By analyzing millions of medical images, AI algorithms can detect even the smallest abnormalities that may be missed by a human doctor. This can be particularly useful in the early detection of diseases such as cancer, where early intervention can be crucial for successful treatment.

AI is also being used to analyze electronic health

records (EHRs) to provide insights into patient care. By combing through vast amounts of patient data, AI algorithms can identify patterns and predict outcomes, allowing healthcare professionals to tailor treatments to individual patients. This can improve patient outcomes while reducing healthcare costs.

Another area where AI is making a significant impact is drug discovery. By analyzing large amounts of data on genetics, disease mechanisms, and potential drug compounds, AI can identify new targets and drug candidates that would be difficult or impossible to identify with traditional methods. This speeds up the drug development process and leads to the discovery of new treatments for previously untreatable conditions.

AI is also used in medical research to uncover new insights into diseases and develop more effective treatments. By analyzing large amounts of data from clinical trials and other research studies, AI can identify new correlations and potential causes of diseases, leading to new treatments and prevention strategies.

Finance

Financial organizations and institutions are using AI to automate complex tasks, enhance customer experience, and identify new opportunities. AI can analyze data faster and more accurately than humans, enabling financial institutions to make better and more informed decisions.

One way in which finance uses AI is in fraud detection. Financial institutions are leveraging machine learning algorithms to analyze patterns in customer transactions and detect fraudulent activity. These algorithms can identify potentially fraudulent transactions, flagging them for further investigation and reducing time and money spent on manual fraud detection.

AI is also being used in investment banking and trading. Machine learning algorithms analyze vast amounts of financial data, including market trends, news articles, and social media sentiment, to predict stock prices and make trading decisions. This also applies to risk management. Machine learning algorithms can identify patterns that suggest potential risks. This helps traders to make better investment decisions and increase their returns.

Customer service

In the world of customer service, companies are constantly looking for ways to improve their interactions with customers, whether it's through phone calls, emails, or online chat. Artificial Intelligence is increasingly important in this area, helping companies provide more efficient and effective customer service.

One of the ways AI is being used in customer service

is through chatbots. Chatbots are computer programs that use natural language processing and machine learning algorithms to understand and respond to customer inquiries. They answer common questions, provide product information, and help customers navigate a company's website.

Another way AI is being used in customer service is through sentiment analysis. This involves using machine learning algorithms to analyze customer feedback and determine the sentiment behind it. For example, a company might use sentiment analysis to determine how customers feel about a new product or service. This information can then be used to improve the product or service or provide customers more personalized support.

AI is also being used to improve the efficiency of customer service operations. For example, AI can automate routine tasks, such as scheduling appointments, sending confirmation emails, or processing refunds. This allows customer service representatives to focus on more complex issues, such as handling customer complaints or resolving technical problems.

Marketing and advertising

Artificial intelligence has revolutionized the way businesses approach marketing and advertising. AI has the ability to analyze vast amounts of data, learn from it, and make accurate predictions, providing insights that can help companies make more informed decisions about their marketing campaigns.

One of the main applications of AI in marketing and advertising is in the field of personalized marketing. By using machine learning algorithms, AI can create detailed customer profiles that include information such as browsing history, purchasing habits, and demographic information. With this information, companies can create personalized marketing campaigns tailored to each customer's specific interests and needs, resulting in more effective marketing and increased customer loyalty.

Another area where AI is making a significant impact in marketing is in the field of content creation. With the help of natural language processing and generation, AI can create high-quality, relevant, and engaging content that resonates with target audiences. This includes everything from social media posts and email campaigns to blog articles and video scripts.

AI is also helping companies optimize their advertising strategies by using predictive analytics to identify the most effective ad placement and targeting strategies. By analyzing user behavior and preferences, AI algorithms can predict which ads are most likely to be clicked, resulting in higher conversion rates and increased return on investment for advertisers.

In addition to personalized marketing and advertising, AI is also used in search engine optimization (SEO). By analyzing search patterns and user behavior, AI algorithms help companies optimize their websites and content to achieve higher search rankings and increase visibility online.

Manufacturing and supply chain management

Artificial Intelligence is transforming manufacturing and supply chain management by optimizing processes and increasing efficiency. In manufacturing, AI is used for quality control, predictive maintenance, and demand forecasting. By analyzing large amounts of data from production lines, AI systems can quickly identify defects or irregularities, allowing for immediate corrective action. Predictive maintenance uses AI algorithms to detect signs of equipment failure before it happens, reducing unplanned downtime and minimizing costs.

AI can also improve supply chain management by real-time inventory tracking, predicting demand, and automating the ordering process. With real-time tracking, companies can quickly adjust their inventory levels to meet demand, reducing the risk of stockouts or excess inventory. Demand forecasting uses historical data and machine learning algorithms to accurately predict demand, allowing companies to optimize their production schedules and reduce inventory holding costs.

Moreover, AI can help companies respond quickly to changing market conditions. By analyzing data from a wide range of sources, including social media and news articles, AI can identify trends and predict shifts in consumer demand, allowing companies to adjust their production and inventory levels accordingly.

Closing Thoughts

We have explored the world of computers and technology, starting from the basic principles of computing and gradually moving on to more advanced topics such as the internet, security, blockchain, and artificial intelligence. We have learned about the history of computers, the different types of computers and their components, how the internet works, and the importance of keeping our online presence secure.

We have also delved into the innovative technology of blockchain, its impact on the financial world and beyond, and how it can create secure and transparent digital transactions. And we have explored the exciting world of artificial intelligence, how it works, and its various real-world applications across various industries.

This book was written with the aim of providing an accessible and comprehensive introduction to computers and technology for those who are new to the subject. We hope that it has been informative and helpful and inspired you to continue exploring the fascinating and ever-evolving world of computing.

It is important to note that the field of computers and technology is constantly evolving, with new developments and innovations emerging all the time. As such, it is essential to stay up-to-date with the latest trends and technologies and to continue learning and exploring this field.

We would like to thank our readers for joining us on this journey, and we hope that this book has provided a solid foundation for further exploration and learning in the exciting and ever-changing world of computers and technology.

lowebooks.com